Oxford International English

Student Anthology

1

OXFORD
UNIVERSITY PRESS

Compiled by
Liz Miles

OXFORD
UNIVERSITY PRESS

Great Clarendon Street, Oxford, OX2 6DP,
United Kingdom

Oxford University Press is a department of the University of Oxford. It furthers
the University's objective of excellence in research, scholarship, and education
by publishing worldwide. Oxford is a registered trade mark of Oxford
University Press in the UK and in certain other countries

© Oxford University Press

British Library Cataloguing in Publication Data
Data available

978-0-19-839215-6

10 9 8 7 6 5 4 3 2 1

Paper used in the production of this book is a natural, recyclable product
made from wood grown in sustainable forests. The manufacturing process
conforms to the environmental regulations of the country of origin.

Printed in Singapore by KHL Printing Co Pte Ltd

Acknowledgements

Cover illustration: Patricia Castelao

Artwork is by: Micha Archer; Alex Brychta; Patricia Castelao; Stefan Chabluk;
Alexandra Colombo; David Dean; Thomas Docherty; Elina Ellis; Jennifer Emery;
Amy Faulkner; Tamara Joubert; Zack Mcloughlin; Alex Steele-Morgan;
John Abbott Nez; Marcin Piwowarski; Bruno Robert; Francois Ruyer; Jan Smith;
Meilo So and Nick Ward

The publishers would like to thank the following for permissions to use their
photographs:

p18: Kaspri/Shutterstock; p18: Fulop Zsolt/Shutterstock; p18: Prapann/
Shutterstock; p18: ScottMurph/Shutterstock; p18: tkemot/Shutterstock;
p18: subarashii21/Shutterstock; p22: SHUTTERSTOCK/manzrussali; p22:
SHUTTERSTOCK/Anna Omelchenko; p22: GETTY/TIM GRAHAM; p22:
SHUTTERSTOCK/Rafal Olechowski; p22: SHUTTERSTOCK/Larisa Lofitskaya;
p22-23: Shutterstock/vic dd; p23: Shutterstock/Andrea Slatter; p48: Willyam
Bradberry/SHUTTERSTOCK; p48: Redchanka/Shutterstock; p49: Yulia Avgust/
SHUTTERSTOCK; p50: Krzysztof Odziomek/SHUTTERSTOCK; p50: Masa
Ushioda/WaterF/AGE FOTOSTOCK; p50: Cardinal/CORBIS; p51: Mark Conlin/
Alamy; p56: AFP/GETTY; p56: Arnold Media/Getty; p57: Richard l'Anson/GETTY;
p57: Terrance Klassen/ALAMY; p58: WGBH Educational Foundation & Stéphane
Bégoin; p58: PhotosIndia.com LLC/ALAMY; p58: LOOK Die Bildagentur der
Fotografen GmbH/ALAMY; p59: Alan Thornton/GETTY; p59: TOLBERT PHOTO/
Alamy; p59: Felipe Oliveira/Dreamstime; p78: Prisma Bildagentur AG/Alamy;
p78-79: Myotis/Shutterstock; p79: bonchan/Shutterstock; p79: Lucinda
Willshire; p85: Boris Stroujko/SHUTTERSTOCK; p88: Keith Leung/ English
Ample School, Hong Kong

The author and publisher are grateful for permission to reprint the following
copyright material:

Yangsook Choi: *The Name Jar* (Dragonfly Books, 2006), copyright © Yangsook
Choi 2001, reprinted by permission of Alfred A Knopf, an imprint of Random
House Children's Books, a division of Ranodm House LLC. All rights reserved.

Thomas Docherty: *Ruby Nettleship and the Ice Lolly Adventure* (Templar, 2010),
copyright © Thomas Docherty 2010, reprinted by permission of Templar
Publishing, an imprint of The Templar Company Ltd. www.templarco.co.uk

John Foster: 'Poppadoms', first published in *Oxford Reading Tree: Food Poems*
compiled by John Foster (OUP, 1993), copyright © John Foster 1993, reprinted
by permission of the author.

D'Arcy Hipgrave: 'My First Year in Vietnam' from *Slurping Soup and other
confusions: true stories and activities to help third culture kids during transition* by
Maryan Afnan Ahmad, Cherie Emigh, Ulrike Gemmer, Barbara Menezes,
Kathryn Tonges and Lucinda Willshire, (2e, Summertime Publishing, 2013),
www.slurpingsoup.com 2010, copyright © 2010 Slurping Soup and Other
Confusions, reprinted by permission of the co-authors.

Richard James: 'Today I'm a Drummer' first published in *Oxford Reading Tree,
Music Poems* compiled by John Foster (OUP, 1996), reprinted by permission of
the author.

Laurie Krebs: *Off We Go To Mexico! An Adventure in the Sun* (Barefoot Books,
2006), text copyright © Laurie Krebs 2006, reprinted by permission of the
publishers.

Liz Miles: 'Puff' from *One, Two, Buckle My Shoe (Magical number Rhymes, old
and new)* (Award Publications, 2006), copyright © Liz Miles 2006, reprinted by
permission of the publishers.

Spike Milligan: 'AB' from *Startling Verse for All the Family* (Michael Joseph, 1987),
copyright © Spike Miligan 1987, reprinted by permission of Spike Milligan
Productions Ltd, at Norma Farnes Management.

Tony Mitton: 'Tiny Diny', copyright © Tony Mitton 2001, from *My Hat and All
That* (Corgi Yearling, 2006), reprinted by permission of David Higham
Associates Ltd for the author.

Jack Prelutsky: 'Late One Night in Kalamazoo' from *Ride a Purple Pelican* (Green
Willow Books, 1986), copyright © Jack Prelutsky 1986, reprinted by permission
of the publishers, HarperCollins Publishers, USA.

Michael Rosen: 'Diggedy-Do' from *Michael Rosen's Book of Nonsense* (Hodder
Children's Books, 2008), copyright © Michael Rosen 1997, reprinted by
permission of Peters Fraser & Dunlop Ltd (www.petersfraserdunlop.com) on
behalf of the author.

Judy Sierra: 'A Hatchling's Song' from *Antarctic Antics: A Book of Penguin Poems*
(Voyager Paperbacks, 2003), text copyright © Judy Sierra 1998, reprinted by
permission of Houghton Mifflin Harcourt Publishing Company. All rights
reserved.

Any third party use of this material, outside of this publication, is prohibited.
Interested parties should apply to the copyright holders indicated in each case.

Although we have made every effort to trace and contact all copyright holders
before publication this has not been possible in all cases. If notified, the
publisher will rectify any errors or omissions at the earliest opportunity.

Contents

A world of stories, poems and facts   4

1 Fiction
New school
The Name Jar   6
by Yangsook Choi

2 Non-fiction
Show me, tell me
Signs and Labels   18
Our Senses   22
How to Make a Spinning
Picture Trick   24

3 Poetry
Everyday poems   30

4 Fiction
Traditional stories
The Magic Paintbrush   36
The Pumpkin in the Jar   44

5 Non-fiction
Water world
Ocean Sharks   48
A–Z of the Sea   52
Sea Transport   56

6 Poetry
Creatures big and small   60

7 Fiction
Fantasy story
Ruby Nettleship and the
Ice Lolly Adventure   66
by Thomas Docherty

8 Non-fiction
About my life
My First Year in Vietnam
was Weird   78
Our Class Trip to the
Animal Park   80
Alex Brychta –
A Biography   84

9 Poetry
Family fun   90

Word Cloud Vocabulary   96

Arctic Ocean

North America

Mexico

USA

Atlantic Ocean

Pacific Ocean

In this book you'll find stories, poems and facts from these countries. Have a look!

South America

The Name Jar

Yangsook Choi

"Are you new here? What's your name?" a girl asked.

"Unhei," said Unhei.

"Ooh-ney?" the girl asked, scrunching up her face.

"Oooh, oooh, oooh-ney!" some kids chanted.

"No, no," Unhei corrected. "It's spelled U–N–H–E–I. It's pronounced Yoon-hye."

"Oh, it's Yoo-hey," the boy said. "Like 'You, hey!' What about 'Hey, you!'"

Just then, the bus pulled up to the school and the doors opened. Unhei hurried to get off.

"You-hey, bye-bye!" the kids yelled as she left. Unhei felt herself blush.

Unhei stood in the doorway of her new and noisy classroom. She was relieved that the kids on the bus had gone to other rooms, but her face still felt red.

"Aren't you going in?" asked a curly-haired boy with lots of dots on his face. "You're the new girl, right?" he asked cheerfully.

Unhei nodded, and before she could walk away, the boy took her hand and pulled her through the door.

"Here's the new girl!" he announced so loudly that the teacher, Mr Cocotos, almost dropped his glasses.

Mr Cocotos thanked him and greeted Unhei.

"Please welcome our newest student," he said to the class. "She and her family just arrived from Korea last week."

Unhei smiled broadly and tried not to show her nervousness.

"What's your name?" someone shouted.

Unhei pictured the kids on the bus. "Um, I haven't picked one yet," she told the class. "But I'll let you know by next week."

As Mr Cocotos showed her to her desk, she felt many round, curious eyes on her.

"Why doesn't she have a name?" she heard someone whisper.

"Maybe she robbed a bank in Korea and needs a new identity," a boy replied.

★ ★

On the bus home, nobody teased her, but Unhei kept thinking about her name.

"How was school, Unhei?" her mother asked when she walked in. "Did you understand the teacher?"

Unhei simply nodded. She unpacked her schoolbag and set the red pouch by a photograph of her grandma.

"I'm glad you are learning English well," her mother said. "You must study hard, behave nicely and get good grades to show that you're a good Korean."

"I will," replied Unhei. "But…I think I would like my own American name," she said quickly.

Her mother looked at her with surprise. "Why? Unhei is a beautiful name. Your grandma and I went to a name master for it."

"But it's *so* hard to pronounce," Unhei complained. "I don't want to be different from all the American kids."

"You *are* different, Unhei," her mother said. "That's a good thing!"

Unhei just wrinkled her nose.

Later that day, Unhei and her mother went grocery shopping in their new neighborhood. They passed Fadil's Falafel, Tony's Pizza and Dot's Deli. A big graffiti-painted garbage truck roared like a lion as it took off down the street. Nothing sounded or looked familiar – until they got to Kim's Market. The sign was in both English and Korean.

Her mother picked up cabbage to make *kimchi* – Korean-style spicy pickled cabbage – and other vegetables and meat. She also found some seaweed, Unhei's favorite, for soup. It made Unhei smile.

"Just because we've moved to America," her mother said, "doesn't mean we stop eating Korean food."

At the checkout counter, a friendly man smiled at Unhei. "Helping your mother with the shopping?" he asked.

Unhei nodded.

"I'm Mr Kim," he said. "And what is your name?"

"Unhei," she answered.

"Ahh, what a beautiful name," he said. "Doesn't it mean *grace*?"

Unhei nodded again. "My mother and grandmother went to a name master for it," she told him.

"A graceful name for a graceful girl," Mr Kim said as he put their groceries into bags. "Welcome to the neighborhood, Unhei."

That evening, Unhei stood in front of the bathroom mirror.

"Hi! My name is Amanda," she said cheerfully. Then she wrinkled her nose.

"Hi! My name is Laura. Hmm. Maybe not…" Her smile turned down. Nothing sounded right. Nothing felt right.

I don't think American kids will like me, she worried as she began to brush her teeth.

"Ha-ee, ma nem id Shoozhy," she said to the mirror with her mouth full of toothpaste.

The next morning, when Unhei arrived at school, she found a glass jar on her desk with some pieces of paper in it. Unhei took one out and read it aloud. "Daisy."

"That's my baby sister's nickname, but she said you can use it if you want," said Cindy, who sat next to her.

Unhei took out the rest of the paper.

"Tamela," she said.

"I got it from a storybook," said Nate. "She was smart and brave."

Unhei nodded and unfolded another piece. "Wensdy?"

"Yeah. You came here on Wednesday," said Ralph.

"Thank you…for your help." A smile spread over Unhei's face.

Ralph quickly said, "We'll put more names in. You can pick whatever you like – or pick them all, and you'll have the longest name in history!"

At three o'clock the bell rang for the end of the school day. Unhei looked out the window and saw it was sprinkling. *It's the same rain,* she thought, *but in a different place.* She watched other kids leaving in groups.

"Hey!" a familiar voice called out to her.

Unhei turned around to see the curly-haired boy again.

"I'm Joey," he said. "And you? Don't you have *any* name?"

Unhei thought for a moment. "Well…I can *show* you," she said, and took out the small red pouch. She pressed the wooden block on the ink pad and then stamped it on a piece of paper. "This is my name stamp," she said. "My grandmother gave it to me… whenever I miss my grandma, I use it to fill a piece of paper."

Word Cloud

curious   neighborhood

favorite   nervousness

identity   relieved

2 Show me, tell me

Signs and Labels

Signs and labels are everywhere. They are on roads, in shops and at school. What signs do you see on the way to school?

Signs tell us where to go.

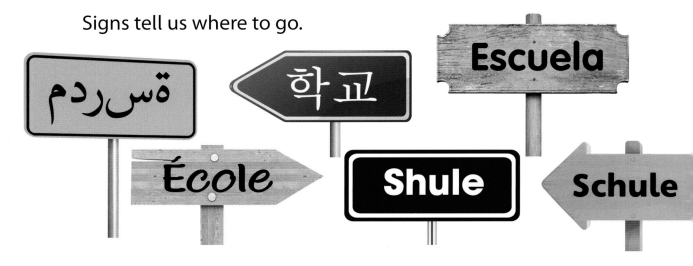

Signs help us cross the road.

Signs warn cars.

Signs show us where to get in.   Signs tell us what to do.

In school, there are lots of signs.

Signs tell us where we must **not** go.

Word Cloud

warn

Signs in the classroom

In the classroom, signs show places to read or paint. Labels help us to find things, like books or paints.

Fire exit

Turn the tap off!

COMPUTER

MATHS

20

Our Senses

We know the world in five ways. We...

1 see

2 hear

3 smell

4 taste

5 touch

These are called the five senses. Parts of our body help us use the five senses. The parts pick up information. The information goes to our brain.

Sight
We see things with our eyes. We see light and colour.

Smell
We smell with our nose. Nostrils in the nose pick up the smells.

Taste
We taste with our tongue. The tongue tells us if food is sweet or sour.

Hearing
We hear with our ears. We can hear quiet sounds and loud sounds.

Touch
We touch and feel things with our hands to find out if they are soft or hard, smooth or rough.

Word Cloud
brain
rough
sour

How to Make a Spinning Picture Trick

A picture trick makes us 'see' something that is not real.

Do the steps to make this spinning picture trick. The spinning picture trick makes us see two pictures as one picture. It puts a lion in a cage!

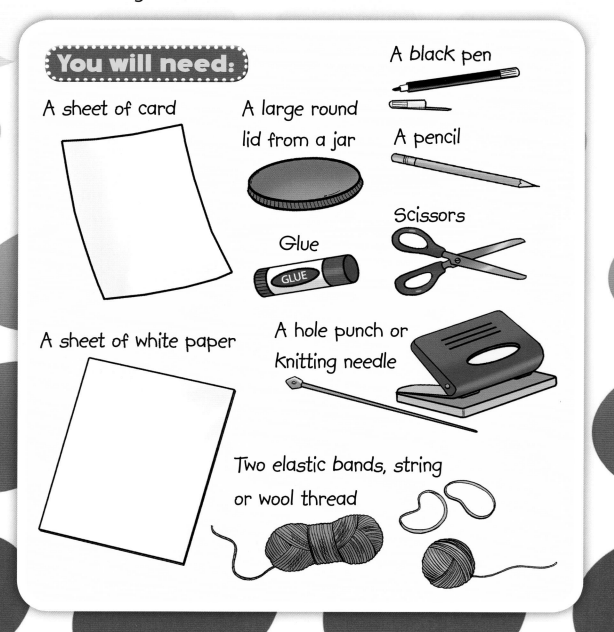

You will need:

A sheet of card

A large round lid from a jar

A black pen

A pencil

Glue

Scissors

A sheet of white paper

A hole punch or knitting needle

Two elastic bands, string or wool thread

Method

1 First, put the jar lid flat on the card. Draw round the lid to make a circle.

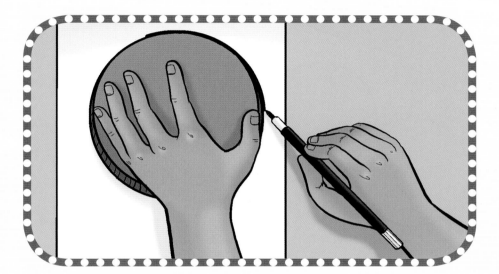

2 Cut out the circle of card.

3 Next, using the jar lid, draw two circles on the sheet of paper. Cut them out.

4 Next, draw a lion in the middle of the first circle of paper. Then, draw a big cage on the second circle of paper. The cage must be bigger than the lion.

Tip
Try drawing in pencil first.

5 Glue the cage picture on one side of the card circle. Glue the lion picture upside down on the other side of the card. Check the cage and lion pictures are opposite ways up.

6 Now make two holes. Use the hole punch or knitting needle to make a hole in each side of the picture. Ask an adult to help you.

7 Put the elastic bands or string through each hole. Loop them so they are fixed to the card.

8 Last, pull the ends of the elastic bands or string and twist. Let them twist back. The circle will whizz. Look at the pictures. Where is the lion?

Try these too

Draw different pictures and glue them on some card. Here are some ideas.

- A bird and a cage

- A duck and a pond

- A spider and a web

- A swimmer and the sea

Word Cloud

loop
opposite
whizz

Diggedy-Do

Diggedy-do
Diggedy-do
The train is late
what shall we do?
Diggedy-do
Diggedy-do
The train is late
what a to-do.
Grandpa coughed
and the wheels fell off.
Diggedy-do
Diggedy-do.

What's the opposite of Diggedy-do?
Diggedy-don't!

Michael Rosen

Word Cloud

to-do

Wobbly Tooth

Wiggerly wibberly
wobberly tooth,
it bibbles and bobbles,
I tell you the truth,
touch with your finger
and you will have proof
of my wiggerly wibberly
wobberly tooth!

John Prior

Word Cloud

bobbles

proof

Today I'm a drummer

Today I'm a drummer,
I'm drumming everywhere,
I'm drumming on the table-top,
I'm drumming on the chair,
I'm drumming on the biscuit tin,
I'm drumming on the bread,
I'll drum my drums till evening comes,
And then I'll drum in bed.

Richard James

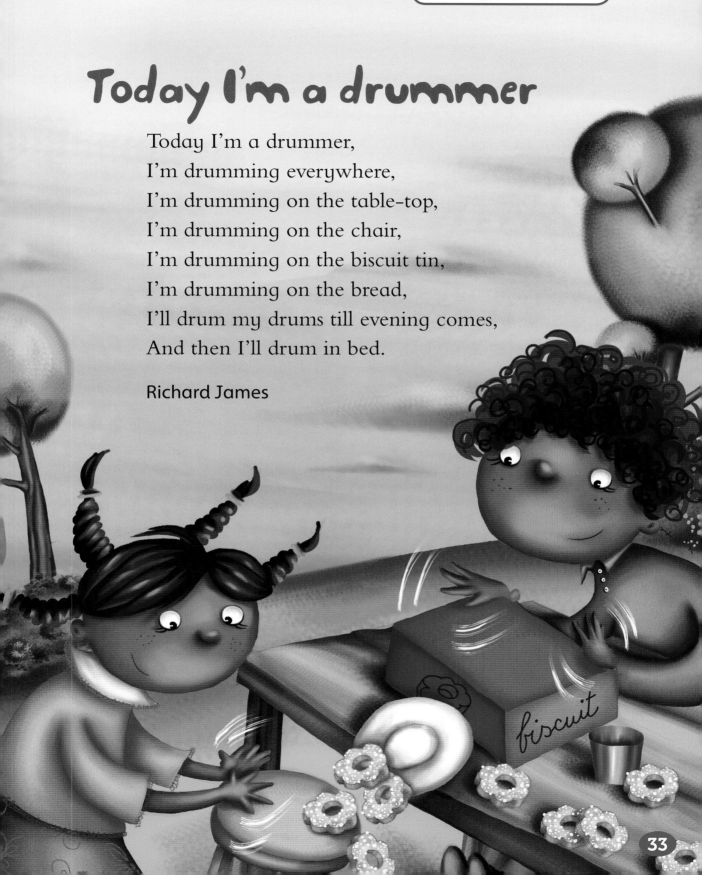

Poppadoms

Poppadoms, poppadoms,
  plain or full of spice.
Poppadoms, poppadoms,
  with chicken and rice.
Crispy hot poppadoms
  to crunch and chew.
A plateful of poppadoms
  just for me and you.

John Foster

Word Cloud

poppadoms

The Magic Paintbrush

A tale from China retold by Liz Miles

Long ago in a tiny village in China lived a young man called Ho. Every day of the year, Ho worked hard on a farm.

Ho looked after the farmer's cows, fed the chickens and cleaned the barns. He dug the fields and planted the seeds.

The farmer was rich but mean. He paid Ho so little for his work, Ho could only buy stale bread to eat. Day by day, Ho became thinner.

Ho was only happy when he was drawing. He drew beautiful pictures on the rocks with chalk. But he wished he could paint colours with a paintbrush.

"If only I had a paintbrush," thought Ho. But Ho was too poor to buy one.

One hot evening when Ho was eating his bread, an old man limped up the lane. The man looked very thin.

"Oh dear," thought Ho, "he looks hungry." Ho was hungry too, but Ho gave the man his bread.

The man thanked him and said, "My friend, you are very kind. Take this. Use it well." He gave Ho a golden paintbrush.

"What a perfect present," said Ho. "Thank you!"

The old man left and Ho soon forgot how hungry he was. "Now all I need are some paints," he thought. So Ho set off through the fields, filling a bucket with plants, berries, rocks and mud.

Ho took the buckets to the little wooden hut where he lived. He tipped the plants, berries, rocks and mud onto the floor.

He ground and mixed the plants, berries, rocks and mud. At last, the berries became red and purple paints. Leaves and flowers became greens, yellows and pinks. Crystals from the rocks became blues and gold. The mud became brown and black.

Soon, Ho had made paints of every colour of the rainbow.

Next, he dipped the paintbrush in the yellow paint. On the wall of the hut he painted a bird. He added feathers of purple and red.

Whoosh! Suddenly, the bird became real! The bird flew out of the window and into the sky – a flash of colour!

"It's a magic paintbrush!" gasped Ho.

Outside, Ho painted a bale of hay for the cows. Whoosh! The hay became real.

The hot summer sun had dried up the river. So, Ho dipped the magic paintbrush in blue and painted a river.

Whoosh! The river became real! People from the village ran to the sparkling water and drank and gulped. The cows lapped. Children swam and splashed.

Everyone cheered as Ho painted some fish. Whoosh! The fish became real and leapt into the water. Hungry fishermen ran to get their fishing rods.

Ho went to the farm. As usual, the farmer was having a great feast – all to himself! He ate and ate, while his workers and their children watched.

"It's not fair," thought Ho.

Ho dipped his brush in the paints and the magic did its work. Soon, there was food for everyone.

Kind Ho used the paintbrush to help the poor. He painted a new wheel for a cart, and pots, pans and new clothes for everyone. "What a clever paintbrush!" said the people. "Thank you, Ho!" cheered the people.

But Ho's good work came to a sudden end. The wicked rich farmer grabbed the magic paintbrush.

"This paintbrush will make me the richest man on Earth," thought the greedy farmer. He painted gold, but nothing happened. He painted jewels. Nothing happened.

"Make the magic work!" yelled the farmer to Ho. "Paint me a mountain of gold."

Ho picked up the magic paintbrush and set to work. He painted an island in a blue sea. On the island he painted a glittering mountain of gold.

Whoosh! The gold and island became real. So did the sea.

The farmer was angry. "How can I get the gold with all that sea? I can't swim! Do something!" he snarled.

Ho painted a sailing ship. The farmer got in the ship and…Whoosh…he floated out to sea.

The farmer steered the ship towards the island of gold. "Soon I shall be the richest man in the world! And all of you will do as I say!" he shouted.

The village people were frightened. But Ho was painting.

Ho painted a storm. Whoosh! The storm became real. Swirling winds blew the ship's sails. The ship went faster. Soon the wicked farmer was carried far, far away.

"We shall never see him again," said Ho.

Everyone sang with joy. Ho painted a party with food, books and toys to celebrate. Whoosh...it all became real.

From that day on, the villagers lived happily, sharing everything. They were not like the greedy farmer.

Ho painted lots of pictures. But they only became real if someone was hungry or sad. The magic paintbrush knew when to work its magic.

Word Cloud

chalk   glittering

crystals lapped

The Pumpkin in the Jar

A tale from the Philippines retold by Liz Miles

Many years ago a king was out hunting for deer. He looked for deer in the forest, while his servants searched the fields.

Amongst the trees, the King saw a little house. A beautiful maiden was outside, watering some pumpkin plants.

"Hello," he said. "I'm very thirsty. May I have some water, please?"

The maiden rushed to the well and filled the only cup she had. It was an old cup. It was chipped and cracked.

"I'm sorry the cup is not fit for a king," she said, "but it is all I have."

The king drank the cool water.

"Thank you," he said and passed the cup back to the maiden. She curtsied, then turned and threw the cup onto the ground. It smashed into hundreds of pieces.

"Why did you do that?" asked the King.

"Now that a great king has drunk from the cup, no one else should," she replied.

The King smiled. His heart was warmed by her kind words.

Back in his palace, the King thought, "The maiden was very kind. I wonder if she is very clever too."

He gave a big jar with a thin neck and tiny top to a servant. "Take this jar to the maiden and give her this message," he said. He whispered the message.

The servant went to the maiden's house. He gave her the large jar with a thin neck and tiny top.

"The King wishes that you bring him a large pumpkin in the jar…but the pumpkin must be whole. It must not be cut into pieces." The servant thought it was an impossible task.

"Easy!" said the maiden. "But it will take me a few months."

Months passed. The King hoped to see the beautiful maiden again. "I wonder if she has solved the problem," he thought.

At last, the maiden came to the palace. She was carrying the jar.

The maiden gave the jar to the King. "I have done as you have asked," she smiled, and then she curtsied.

"Let's see," he smiled. The King turned and dropped the jar on the ground. It smashed and a large, orange pumpkin rolled across the floor!

The King was overjoyed. "Dear maiden, you are clever! Please, will you marry me?" And he bowed.

The maiden agreed to marry him, and the clever King and Queen lived very happily together forever.

One day, the servant went to his Queen and asked, "How did you get the pumpkin into the jar?"

She laughed and showed him some pumpkin seeds. "I put one of these in the jar with some soil. I watered it every day. A pumpkin grew and the jar was soon full!"

"You are clever," said the servant.

Word Cloud
curtsied
maiden
warmed

Water world

Ocean Sharks

What is a shark?

A shark is a fish. Sharks swim in seas all over the world. Some sharks swim in cold seas, some prefer warm seas. Some sharks live close to the shore. Some live in deep seas.

Parts of a shark

A shark has a tail and fins for swimming. The tail beats the sea to push it along. The tail and fins help steer it and stop it from rolling over.

Sharks have a strong sense of smell but cannot see very far.

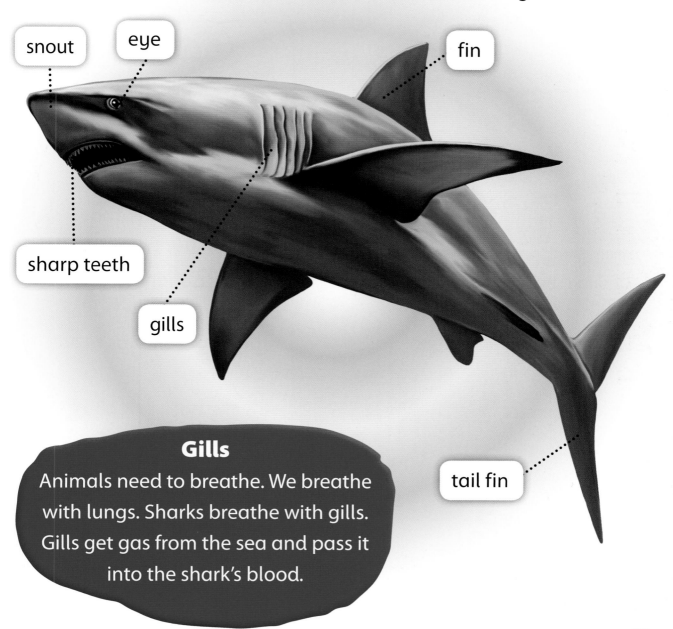

snout

eye

fin

sharp teeth

gills

tail fin

Gills

Animals need to breathe. We breathe with lungs. Sharks breathe with gills. Gills get gas from the sea and pass it into the shark's blood.

All sorts of sharks

There are many different sorts of sharks.

Sharks can be as long as a truck or shorter than an arm. Two of the biggest sharks are the whale shark and the basking shark. The dwarf lantern shark is the smallest. It fits in a person's hand.

whale shark

basking shark

dwarf lantern shark

Glossary

fin a flat bit that sticks out from the body or tail of a fish

fish a creature that lives in water, has fins and breathes using gills

hunter a shark or creature that kills fish or other sea creatures to eat their flesh

tail the back end of a fish's body. The tail fin helps it to swim

Shark attack!

We fear some sharks, but some sharks are harmless. The whale shark is a gentle giant – it does not attack.

The great white shark is the biggest hunter in the sea. It hunts seals and penguins. It hunts other sharks too and can attack people. If a shark is spotted near a beach, swimmers rush to land.

Hunting sharks have hundreds of teeth set in rows. They are very sharp and pointed.

Word Cloud

flesh   lungs

harmless   shore

hunts

51

A–Z of the Sea

Aa

albatross

A large bird with long wings that can fly far across oceans.

anemone

An animal that lives on coral and in rock pools and looks like a plant.

Arctic Ocean

The world's smallest ocean around the cold North Pole.

(Look at the world map on page 55 to see all the oceans of the world.)

Bb

baleen whale

A kind of whale that does not have teeth. It has lots of soft plates in its mouth (called baleen) which hang down and allow food to pass through them.

baleen

bay

A part of the sea that cuts into the land.

beach

Land by the sea made of sand or pebbles.

blubber

Fat under the skin of seals and other sea animals that keeps them warm in cold seas and on cold coasts.

Cc

cave

A big hole in a cliff.

cliff

A steep hill made of rock next to the sea.

coast

The land that is right next to the sea.

cliff

beach

coral

A type of rock in the sea that is made from the skeletons of tiny creatures.

cove

A small bay.

crab

An animal that has a hard shell on its back and powerful claws, which lives in the sea.

crocodile

A large animal that lives in rivers and along coasts in some countries.

current

A mass of sea water that moves in one direction.

Dd

dolphin

A large mammal that swims like a fish, breathes air and does not have gills.

dugong

A mammal that lives in the Pacific and Indian Oceans and is called a 'sea cow' because it eats grass under the water.

Oceans of the world

Word Cloud

claws	mass
direction	oceans
mammal	skeletons

For fun with dictionaries go to
www.oxforddictionaries.com/words/free-primary-resources

Sea Transport

There are lots of ways to travel across the sea. Some ways have been used for a long time and some are new.

Paddling

Paddling is the oldest form of crossing the water. Thousands of years ago people made boats from big logs or tree trunks. They made paddles to push the boat along.

paddle

dugout canoe

Kayaks

Lots of people paddle small boats today. Many kayaks are made from a type of plastic. Sea kayaks are good for exploring caves along the coast.

a sea kayak

Dragon boats

Dragon boats were first made 2,000 years ago in China. They are made from wood. A team of paddlers make dragon boats move fast.

Each boat has a carved dragon head at the front.

This is a dragon boat race at Stanley Beach, Hong Kong. A crowd of 30,000 people watch the race each year.

Sailing

Ancient Egyptians and Arabs were the first people to use sails to power their boats and ships.

These days, sailing is a very popular sport and hobby.

sail

4,500 years ago Ancient Egyptians used boats like this to sail across the sea.

57

Biggest

Today, the biggest sailing ships are called tall ships. They are sailed in races and take holidaymakers on trips.

The *Royal Clipper* has five masts and lots of sails.

mast

sail

The *Royal Clipper* is like a palace inside.

Fastest

Skilled sailors race small sailing boats across oceans. Some of the fastest sailing boats are called catamarans. They have two hulls.

You have to be fit to sail a boat fast.

two hulls

Wacky invention

The sailors on this boat can relax. But is it a boat? It looks just like a car.

An amphicar

Answer: It is both! This car-boat can travel on a road and drive into the sea!

An engine drives the wheels on the road. In the sea, the engine drives a propeller.

A **propeller** is a set of spinning blades that pushes a boat along.

Word Cloud

carved	hull
dugout canoe	power (verb)
engine	skilled

Puff!

One puff, two puffs, three puffs, four
Five puffs, six puffs –
You can't see me any more!

Liz Miles

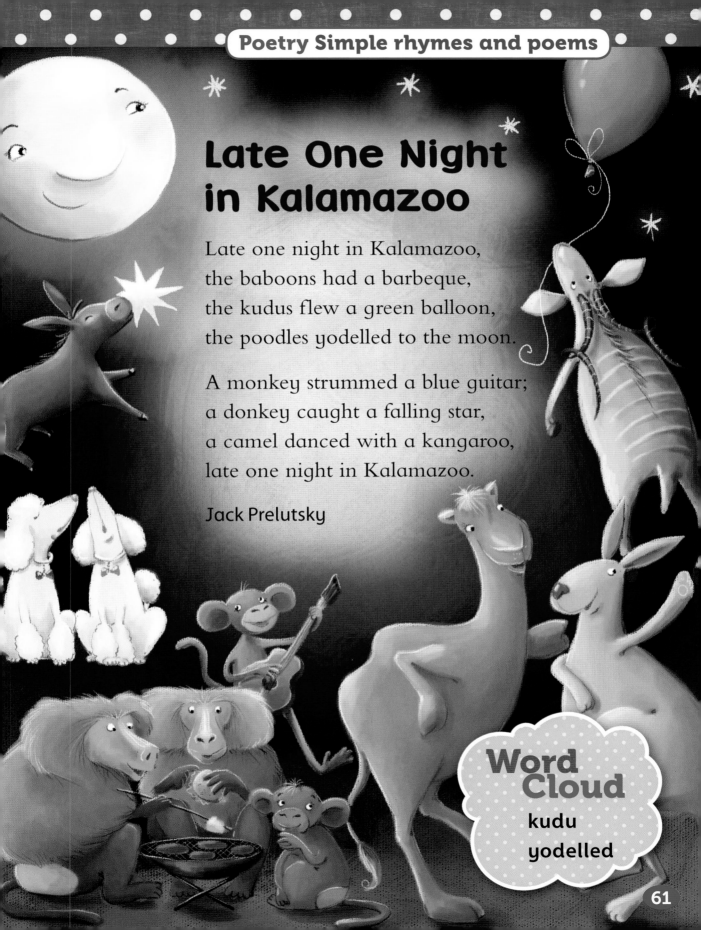

Late One Night in Kalamazoo

Late one night in Kalamazoo,
the baboons had a barbeque,
the kudus flew a green balloon,
the poodles yodelled to the moon.

A monkey strummed a blue guitar;
a donkey caught a falling star,
a camel danced with a kangaroo,
late one night in Kalamazoo.

Jack Prelutsky

Word Cloud
kudu
yodelled

A Hatchling's Song

I'm almost hatched!
I'm almost hatched!
I'm small, I'm wet,
I'm not out yet.
I'm almost hatched!

I'm pecking hard,
I'm pecking hard.
I'm tired, I'm weak,
It hurts my beak.
I'm pecking hard.

My head's outside,
My head's outside.
The moon is bright –
The world's so white!
My head's outside.

I'm really hatched,
I'm really hatched.
At last I'm free.
Hey, Dad, it's me!
I'm really hatched.

Judy Sierra

A B

A Bee!
  A Bee!!
    Is after me!!!
      And that is why
    I flee!!!!
   I flee!!!!!
  This bee
This bee
  Appears to be
  Very very
    ANG
      -ER
       -REE!!!!

Spike Milligan

Tiny Diny

Dear, oh dear,
oh, what shall I do?
There's a tiny little dinosaur
in my shoe.

Her teeth are sharp
and her head's like a rock
When I put my foot in,
she chewed my sock.

Her skin is rough
and her tail is long.
And her ripply muscles
are ever so strong.

And I want to go out,
but what can I do
with a tiny little dinosaur
in my shoe?

Tony Mitton

Word Cloud

muscles

ripply

Ruby Nettleship and the Ice Lolly Adventure

Thomas Docherty

This is Ruby Nettleship.

She likes climbing and sliding and running and jumping, and when she isn't doing any of these things, she is dreaming of adventures.

In the park by Ruby's house there was an old, falling-apart playground. The slide didn't slide, the roundabout wouldn't go round and the see had lost its saw.

The only thing that worked was the swing, and there was always a big queue of children waiting to swing on it.

One hot afternoon, Ruby and her friends had been waiting for ages…

...when CRASH!

The swing came un-swung.

Now there was NOTHING to play on and the children began to wander home.

"Come on, let's go," called Ruby's friends.

But something about the playground made Ruby want to stay.

Without the other children, the playground felt sadder than before.

"No one cares," mumbled Ruby to herself, as she tugged at the broken swing. "If this was my playground there would be loads of brilliant stuff for EVERYONE to play on…"

But just then she was interrupted by the tinkle of an ice cream van. It drew up right next to Ruby.

"Not many people today," remarked the lady in the van cheerfully.

"The swing broke," explained Ruby.

"Well that won't do," said the lady. "Here, have an ice lolly."

And she handed Ruby a lolly in a green wrapper.

"It's my last one."

Ruby took the lolly. "Thank you," she remembered to say, but when she looked up again the ice cream van had vanished.

"That's strange," thought Ruby, turning her attention to the lolly.

It was green like the wrapper, but it seemed to glow from the inside.

She took a bite. It tasted delicious, so she took another one. The letters 'P' and 'L' appeared on the end of the lolly stick.

71

Ruby ate the rest of the lolly quickly and held the stick up to examine it. It read:

PLANT ME

"I wonder what will happen if I do?" thought Ruby.

No one was about, so she pushed the lolly stick firmly into the ground, covered it up and waited.

Almost immediately Ruby felt a rumbling in the ground beneath her.

She watched in amazement as a multicoloured shoot pushed its way up through the soil.

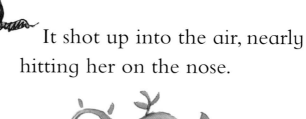

It shot up into the air, nearly hitting her on the nose.

Once it had grown to twice Ruby's height, it sprouted new branches that twisted and turned into a beautiful swing.

"Wow!" cried Ruby. She climbed aboard and launched herself into the air.

As Ruby started to swing, more shoots appeared. They quickly sprouted ladders and poles that blossomed and bloomed with swings and slides.

Ruby was swinging so high by now that she could see over the whole city. "I bet no one else is having this much fun," she thought to herself.

Then Ruby had an idea.

As if it had read her thoughts, the playground flowered over the whole park and began to spill out into the street.

The first thing Ruby did was to pick up her friends and all the other children who lived nearby.

"This way!" shouted Ruby, and with that, they headed off towards town.

On the way, they dropped in at the ZOO…
to see if the animals wanted to come out and play.

After that, they visited the supermarket…
and made a GIANT trolley roller coaster.

By the time they got into the centre of town, the playground was full to bursting. Even the grown-ups had climbed out of their cars, put down their shopping, forgotten about work and joined in the fun.

Soon, the whole city had ground to a halt.

"NOW WHAT?" wondered Ruby.

Word Cloud

launched

queue

sprouted

tinkle

My First Year in Vietnam was Weird

D'Arcy Hipgrave (aged 7)

from *Slurping Soup and Other Confusions: www.slurpingsoup.com*

When I left Melbourne in Australia to live in Hanoi in Vietnam it was really weird. I missed the traffic lights in Melbourne. There were no traffic lights in Hanoi, so mad motorbikes were everywhere, even on the footpaths!

Traffic in Hanoi

Me, in noisy Hanoi!

Another thing I missed was playing footy. In Hanoi, I started Tae Kwon Do. But I wanted to be a footy player when I was older.

On my first day at school, my brother and I went by cyclo. The cyclo was a bit like a baby pram. I felt shy at school. I didn't like the first year.

Me on a trip to Sapa in northern Vietnam

In the second year I went to a French school. But learning to speak French was hard, so I wanted to go back to the English school. I think I was a bit mixed up.

Later on that year, I met Jono, another Aussie. My French got better, and then I felt very happy.

Now I have a black belt in Tae Kwon Do. I can speak French and some Vietnamese. I love Vietnamese food, especially *pho*. I have friends from Vietnam and many other countries. Vietnam is my home and it is not at all weird.

Vietnamese *pho* soup

Word Cloud

Aussie	Melbourne
footy	Tae Kwon Do
Hanoi	Vietnamese

Our Class Trip to the Animal Park

Welcome to Hippo-Happy Wildlife Park

Last Friday, Mrs Tang and Mr Khan took our class on a trip. We went to the Animal Park.

We got to school at 8 o'clock to get on the coach. We had to bring a drink and a snack for lunch. Mrs Tang soon got cross because Rosa was late. The coach had to wait ten more minutes.

At last, the coach set off. We all sang songs. We were happy until Rosa spilled her drink. Mr Khan cleaned the floor then I helped Rosa clean her hands. After singing lots more songs, Rosa and I played I-spy.

At 9 o'clock the coach got to the Animal Park. First, a woman told us we must not get too near to the animals. Then she told us to respect the animals and be careful not to upset them.

Park Rules
Stay with your adult.
Do not enter the animal enclosures.
Do not throw objects at any animals.
Do not try to kiss the animals.

Next, we split into two groups. Rosa and I went in Mrs Tang's group. After going up lots of steps we saw the lions. The lions lay on the grass and then one got up and roared. It had sharp teeth, so I was happy to be up the tower. After a short walk from the tower, we saw a tiger too.

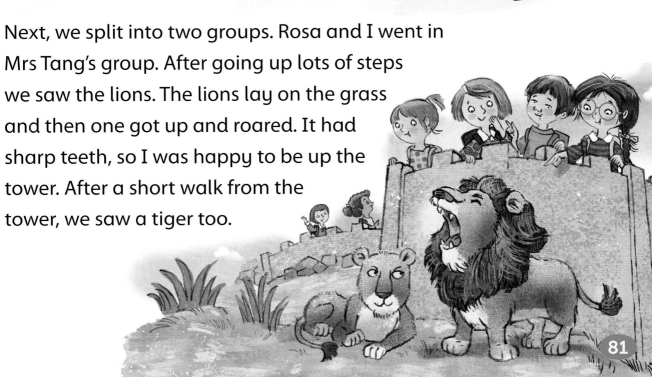

81

Then we saw the giraffes. When the park warden let us feed a baby giraffe, Rosa jumped because it licked her arm.

At lunchtime, we all sat near the lake. After eating lunch we went to a shack for ice creams. Next, we followed signs to the bathrooms.

During the afternoon we went to see the hippos in the mud, then the pandas. The last thing we visited was the insects and big spiders! The warden let Leroy hold a big beetle for a minute.

Finally, we went into a shop. I got a panda balloon. Rosa got a plastic spider. At first, Mrs Tang screamed at the spider, but then Rosa told her it was plastic.

While we waited for the coach we played on swings and slides. At last the coach roared into the coach park. We jumped in and it took us back.

We got to school at 4 o' clock. We thanked the driver and our teachers before we went home.

It was a brilliant day. I liked the hippos best but Rosa's plastic spider was fun, too.

Word Cloud

enclosures
respect

Alex Brychta – a Biography

Introduction

Alex Brychta is a very clever illustrator. He draws and paints pictures for stories. The stories are about three children, called Bif Chip and Kipper. They have a dog called Floppy. Lots of children read the stories and love Alex's illustrations.

Alex in his art studio.

How did Alex get his job? Why do children love his illustrations? Read about his life to find out …

Alex Brychta has illustrated hundreds of books. He has drawn Floppy the dog 30,000 times!

Biff (girl) has a twin brother called Chip. Kipper is their younger brother.

Alex's childhood

Alex was born in 1956 in Czechoslovakia. Today, the country is called the Czech Republic.

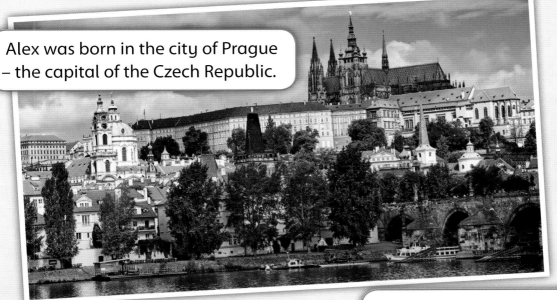

Alex was born in the city of Prague – the capital of the Czech Republic.

Alex's parents were artists, so Alex did lots of drawing as a little boy. When he was older he drew cartoons.

Alex was ten years old when he did this cartoon.

Three-year-old Alex

85

A new country

In 1968, Czechoslovakia was invaded by another country called the Soviet Union. Army tanks rolled down the streets. Tanks came into Alex's school grounds, too! Alex's mum and dad were very upset. They told Alex and his sister that they must leave Czechoslovakia.

One night, the family packed their bags and set off in the car. They went on small, quiet roads, so that the soldiers did not stop them. After a long journey, the family got to England to start a new life. Alex was twelve years old.

The family escaped from Czechoslovakia.

North Sea

England

Czech Republic

It was a long journey to England.

In England

At first, Alex could not understand English. He drew lots of pictures at school and did not listen to the teachers. A teacher told him off. But the teacher looked at his drawings. He said, "Alex, these are very good and look like book illustrations."

First jobs

Alex's first job was a book about Spain. He was sixteen. His career as an illustrator had started.

Alex with his sister, mum and dad in England.

87

Biff, Chip, Kipper and Floppy

In 1984, the author Rod Hunt wanted an illustrator for his Biff, Chip and Kipper books. He liked Alex's illustrations. He asked Alex to draw Biff, Chip, Kipper and Floppy.

In July, Alex illustrated the first story about Biff, Chip and Kipper. It was called *A New Dog*, so Floppy was in it too!

Next, he illustrated 23 more stories by Rod! In 1986, 24 stories were published and sold to schools. The books were popular and read by children in the UK. Later, children in lots of countries started reading Rod and Alex's books.

The stories were very popular, so the publisher asked Rod and Alex to write lots of new stories.

Children around the world love the Oxford Reading Tree books.

Family life

In 1989, Alex married Dina. They had two children, Kelly and Dylan. When Kelly and Dylan were young, they helped their father illustrate two of his books.

500 books!

In 2012, Alex and Rod were each given a special award by Queen Elizabeth II of Great Britain. Alex was very proud of this award but he said, "The best thing is that all over the world millions of children enjoy reading our books."

By 2013, Alex had illustrated over 500 Oxford Reading Tree books. His books are sold in 136 countries. The stories are in nine different languages.

Word Cloud

cartoons
illustrator
published
Soviet Union

Off We Go to Mexico!

Laurie Krebs

Off we go, off we go, off we go to Mexico!

We swim in turquoise water and build castles on the beach.
We climb up rocks or watch from docks,
To see the grey whales breach.

We hop aboard the canyon train. Across the bridge we go.
Up mountains steep, through tunnels deep,
We dare not look below.

We hurry to a festival held in the village square.
There's food to eat and friends to meet
And laughter everywhere.

We climb amazing pyramids from ancient Mexico
And wonder how they're standing now
When built so long ago.

We tap our feet to music by the mariachi bands,
Who strum guitars beneath the stars
And sing, as we clap hands.

We trek to native villages, for this is market day.
Their rich supply of things to buy
Creates a bright display.

We circle round the plaza and we hear the stamping feet.
As dancers twirl, their costumes swirl
To the guitarists' beat.

We hike up to the winter home of the monarch butterflies.
When sunshine brings a burst of wings,
Their glitter fills the skies.

We wave our flags, green, white and red. Parades are under way.
As floats pass by, flares fill the sky.
It's Independence Day!

We wander through the capital, where there's so much to see:
The park, the zoo, museums too,
And Aztec history.

But now our trip is over and it's time to say farewell.
So home we go from Mexico –
We've got so much to tell!

Word Cloud

Aztec   mariachi
bands   trek
breach   twirl
flares
Independence
  Day

95

Word Cloud

A

Aussie

Aztec

B

bands

bobbles

brain

breach

C

cartoons

carved

chalk

claws

crystals

curious

curtsied

D

direction

dugout canoe

E

enclosures

engine

F

favorite

flares

flesh

footy

G

glittering

H

Hanoi

harmless

hull

hunts

I

identity

illustrator

Independence
 Day

K

kudu

L

lapped

launched

loop

lungs

M

maiden

mammal

mariachi

mass

Melbourne

muscles

N

neighborhood

nervousness

O

oceans

opposite

P

poppadoms

power

proof

published

Q

queue

R

relieved

respect

ripply

rough

S

shore

skeletons

skilled

sour

Soviet Union

sprouted

T

Tae Kwon Do

tinkle

to-do

trek

twirl

V

Vietnamese

W

warmed

warn

whizz

Y

yodelled

Spalding
in the Fifties

SPALDING
Guardian

at heart  publications

First Published in 2007 by:
At Heart Ltd, 32 Stamford Street, Altrincham,
Cheshire, WA14 1EY.

in conjunction with

Spalding Guardian & Lincolnshire Free Press
Priory House, The Crescent, Spalding, PE11 1AB

Printed by Bell & Bain, Scotland.

ISBN: 978 1 84547 158 3

Introduction 4

Agriculture and Industry 6

Scenic Views 20

Children 27

Sport 56

Civic and Leisure 69

Best of the Rest 108

Introduction

HAULIERS were facing bankruptcy as petrol rationing continued, while farmers were struggling with drought-ridden crops, and traders were battling with the council about the price of car parking.

These were some of the stories hitting Spalding's headlines in 1957, although you could easily be mistaken for thinking they came out of more recent editions of the *Lincolnshire Free Press*.

When I first started the task of going back through the archives to choose the pictures which appear in this book, I couldn't help but think how different things were then when compared to the present day.

Everything from the clothes people wore, the things they did and the homes they lived in seemed poles apart from today's norm, if there is such a thing.

In 1957 Herbert Butcher was the area's MP, Spalding's ratepayers faced bills of 18 shillings, and the *Lincolnshire Free Press* cost threepence while the wind turbines which now dominate parts of the Fenland skyline were not even a twinkle in developers' eyes.

Since then the world has become smaller due to advancements in technology, transport, medical practices and the invention of the Internet.

Things have changed a great deal in the past 50 years but as I continued my step back in time and looked at the papers more closely I realised that the stories told then are perhaps not so different to those which are featured today.

Instead of appearing on Ready, Steady Cook, *Lincolnshire Free Press* readers were showing off their culinary skills on Woman's Hour.

And rather than taking on the Three Peaks Challenge, people were swimming the Coronation Channel as they sought to stretch themselves physically.

Life may have been simpler, but no doubt for many living off the land in a small south Lincolnshire market town it was a lot harder as well.

But people were fighting the same issues – a classic example is car park prices in Spalding.

Traders said the fees were putting them under massive strain and allied together through the chamber of trade to fight Spalding Urban Council.

This story has come full circle in 2007 with the traders of Holbeach locked in a battle with South Holland District Council about the same issue in their town today.

1957 was an important year on the world stage too. It was the year the Rome Treaty was signed establishing the common market, Sputnik was launched into space by the Russians and Bridge on the River Kwai picked up the Oscar for best film.

Some of the bigger stories of the year in Spalding included proposals for the development of a sports centre on the Castle Fields.

New secondary schools at Spalding, Holbeach, Long Sutton and Deeping St James were all under construction.

Hovenden House, at Fleet, was handed over by the Worth family to become a Leonard Cheshire Home.

And Tulips' manager Don Pickwick took his boys to Durham, for the first round proper of the FA Cup.

Many of these are featured on the pages of this book.

I love the quirky, interesting tales – those which feature a real character who has a story to tell and many of those also appear in the following pages.

Among my favourites is local strong-man Carl Danes, who at 67 years of age hammered a two-inch nail through six-inches of wood in two minutes – using his bare hands!

And two Spalding schoolboys who holed themselves up in a mystery workshop and set about building themselves a full-sized plane.

As I started out deciding how to organise the photos I noticed that the majority of them neatly fell into several different categories.

The first of these is agriculture and industry.

Agriculture has been the staple of Spalding and its surrounding district for as long as anyone can remember and I believe it always will be.

Many of the pictures in our editions, even to day, feature people toiling on the land, whether it be picking or planting vegetables or cropping flowers.

The pictures featured in this section will no doubt recall many memories for those who devoted their life to working the area's rich land.

And they provide a great record of the advancements in machinery and methods along the way.

The next section is devoted to the areas beautiful landscapes and scenic shots captured by staff photographers.

I am sure, if you know where to look, many of these beauty spots can still be found, unspoilt.

These pictures show just what an amazing part of the countryside we live in and perhaps, one we all too often take for granted.

Children are the subject of the third chapter.

As is still the case today the youngsters of Spalding and the surrounding area are a key feature of local newspapers.

They were, as they are today often snapped at school, taking part in plays or with youth group, such as the scouts and guides.

Civic events and rural pastimes is the subject of the fourth area featured – this covers a multitude of events and traditions, many of which are still followed today.

The hallowed contest to find Miss Tulip Land 1957 and the Tulip Time festivities themselves make up much of this chapter, along with the exchange visits made between representatives of Spalding and its German twin-town Speyer, endless church and parish fetes plus village celebrations.

The achievements of our sporting folk are the subject of the next chapter.

It was an important year for Spalding Town, who made it to the FA Cup first round, but there are numerous other teams, clubs and societies who made their way into the pages of the *Lincolnshire Free Press* and its sister paper the *Spalding Guardian*.

The best of the rest brings this pictorial treasure trove of life in Spalding to a close.

It is made up of those character stories, events and moments which were caught on camera, including when Spalding's Market Place cobblestones disappeared for the last time and when a motor mechanic became the envy of his friends by building his own sports car.

I just hope you get as much pleasure out of looking through the pages of this book as I did choosing the pictures to compile it.

Kate Chapman
Senior reporter
Spalding Guardian and Lincolnshire Free Press
(2007)

Agriculture and Industry

■ While most people were snug by the fireside on Boxing Day, the work of taking the sugar beet to the Spalding factory went on in bitter weather and the first snow of winter. These lorries wait their turn while drivers shiver in the road. (f3850)

■ And one trailer came to grief on the icy road. (f3853)

■ The Deeping Fen Drainage Board started work on its new pumping station in 1956. This shot shows the work completed up to February, 1957. The facility would have three electric pumps once finished. (g198)

Mild weather caused a glut of flowers on the markets. These workers were snapped cropping a fine show of William Copeland tulips at Mssrs H Neal and Son, in Monkshouse Lane, Spalding. (g346)

There were still thousands of tons of potatoes in their clamps on farms in south Lincolnshire.. During the summer-like spell potato riddling for the markets was in progress on a few farms, including this one at Wragg Marsh, in Spalding. (g743)

It was the same story from flower growers all over the area – daffodil prices hit rock bottom and were the lowest ever known.

It was reported that the flowers hardly paid for picking – but they had to be cleared. This picture taken at Surfleet was typical of activity through the district. (g812)

A worker picks watercress at Bourne after harvesting it from Spalding Urban Council's watercress beds. The harvest was eagerly awaited in 1957 because of the weather and it was the best harvest at Bourne since 1950. (g767)

■ It was flat out activity on the land in April with potato setting predominant. This typical scene was captured in the Spalding Marsh area. (g1020)

■ When this photograph was taken firemen and farmers had been working 36 hours to pull this burning fodder stack to pieces. It was on the farm of Mr J. R. Bishop, Moulton Eaugate. (g2532)

■ 'Shop in Spalding' was the theme of the town's trade fair. Angela Pask (8), daughter of one of the organisers, presented a bouquet to Mrs Dryden after the opening of the spring fair. (g1029)

■ The appliance of science: Visitors to Smedley's canning factory are shown some of the hi-tech machinery in action with these three other images on this page. (g1149-51)

■ Cheers: Some of the women workers who were among the 200 guests at Smedley's annual dinner. This year's dinner was held at the Spalding Corn Exchange. (g376)

■ Farmers from a wide area flocked to a 12-acre field belonging to Mr J. D. Mawby to see a new plough demonstrated. Here they are shown examining the Bonnel one-way, three-furrow trailing plough in great detail. (g1333)

■ Coming along swimmingly: Work on the county's first school swimming pool at Donington was well underway. The 75ft facility at the Cowley Secondary School was funded by the Cowley Foundation. (g1205)

■ Making headway: The new Long Sutton secondary modern school was expected to be open by Christmas or early spring. New secondary schools were also underway in Spalding, Deeping St James (g1221) and Holbeach (g1131), below.

■ Typical Tulip Time weather: A man with his coat collar turned up against the chill wind watches as tulips are cut for market at Weston. (g1137)

■ "It needs no words of mine to praise the shopping services of Spalding. For a town of its size Spalding does not play second fiddle to anyone in that connection." These were the comments of the newly elected Spalding Urban Council chairman Coun C. H Peck, after opening Spalding's Trade Exhibition. (g1667)

The grand parade of horses and cattle at Deeping Show in June. (g1782)

A little boy tries out a tractor for size at the annual Deeping Show. (g1789)

■ Histon Lassie 4th, a percheron owned by Mr H. E. Sneath, of West Pinchbeck, won first prize in the Suffolk/Percheron class. (g1787)

■ One of the highlights in the sweltering heat at Long Sutton Agricultural Show were the horse jumping events. A young rider clears a fence in the juvenile round. This was the 10th annual post-war show. (g2211)

■ Farm turnouts class at Long Sutton Agricultural Show come for a lot of admiration from the crowd. (g2215)

■ Yields of peas in July 1957 were reported to be very heavy. This picture shows workers loading up pea straw on a south Lincs farm. (g2225)

86 years young: Alderman G. W. Chatterton, of Fulney House, Spalding, works on the land with his son Mr Hugh Chatterton and his grandsons Hugh (16) and Ian (15). (g2674)

The scene of Spalding sugar beet factory working night and day to deal with the south Lincolnshire beet crop was a familiar one in October. The campaign generally lasted until the end of January and farmers experienced ideal weather for lifting in 1957. (g3122)

Spalding Chamber of Trade's Autumn fair suffered due to illness and bad weather, but attracted record attendance on the final day. It was opened by MP Sir Herbert Butcher. (g3248)

An exceptional mangold yields of 80 tons per acre with some of the roots weighing three stone each, was grown by Mr J Read, of Glebe Farm, Horbling Fen. (g3485)

Scenic Views

■ This traditional Boxing Day hunt scene is becoming increasingly rare. Our photographer caught the Cottesmore Hunt on film as it set off across the rolling countryside at Dunsby. (f3863)

■ June-like weather in March brought spring to the countryside early. The flowers were in full bloom and foliage was developing in this beauty spot at Pinchbeck Marsh. (g753)

■ As well as the colourful tulip fields, the countryside in the Spalding district was looking at its best in its new spring garb. This beautiful scene was found at Weston. (g1242)

With summer around the corner gypsies were taking to the road again – bearing along with their centuries old atmosphere of tranquility. This picturesque scene as a caravan passes through was taken at Pinchbeck. (g1739)

Standing among the trees in a lovely Weston Lane were the remains of a once beautiful manor house – St Lambert's Hall, which was demolished because the owners had no use for it. The house had fallen into a bad state of disrepair as no-one had lived in it since 1950 when it was a hostel. Before that it belonged to the late Mr George Caudwell. (g1673)

■ Geronimo! The banks of the River Glen at Pinchbeck proved a popular spot with local bathers during the hot weather. Pinchbeck Swimming Club worked hard to develop this stretch of the bank – providing a spring board, temporary changing hut and wooden staging. (g2103)

■ The beauty of Wykeham Abbey was captured by a *Lincolnshire Free Press* photographer with this photograph on a crisp autumn day. (g3367)

■ The fall of the year had begun. The leaves on the trees had taken on golden hints and other rainbow hues and many were shed as the days became shorter. This shot captures Moulton's stately parish church. (g3234)

■ Step back in time: The Marquis of Exeter's hounds meet at Bourne in an olde world setting provided by the Manor House home of Mr and Mrs E. D. Cook in The Austerby. (g3917)

■ Up close and personal: Two youngsters came across this bushy-tailed squirrel as went about his daily business with confident aerobics in his home, at Ayscoughfee Gardens, in Spalding. (g213/4)

Children

■ He's behind you! Members of Holbeach Youth Club entertain audiences with their annual Christmas pantomime. This year's offering was the colourful tale of *Sinbad the Sailor*. (g13)

■ Smile! A row of young, happy faces greeted our cameraman when he turned up at the annual January party at St John's Primary School in Spalding. (g24)

■ Jamboree time: Spalding Scouts were among the guests at a special party thrown by the Second Spalding Guides. More than 70 youngsters enjoyed the fun and games at Moose Hall. (g169)

'What's all the fuss about?' asked Sutton Bridge children Maureen (8) and John Kilbon when they were collected from a friend's house by their sister. The pair had been playing hide and seek all day and did not know the police had been called and an appeal for their whereabouts broadcast at a local cinema. (g263)

These delightful scenes were taken at the pantomime *Dick Whittington and his Cat*, presented by the Local Girls' Friendly Society, at Long Sutton. Dainty youngster Jane Williamson showed off her pirouettes during her ballet performance (top). (g297/8)

■ The Fenland Tappers were no strangers to treading the boards and the young troop was well known throughout the district. The girls are pictured here after another fine performance at Whaplode St Catherine. (g229)

■ These next three pictures feature youngsters who tripped the light fantastic during a dancing festival at Holbeach. Children from Gedney Dyke, Holbeach and Sutton Bridge donned their glad rags for the occasion. (g819/20/21)

■ Spalding Scouts, Cubs, Guides and Brownies valiantly marched through Love Lane on their way to the parish church for a commemorative service. They were going to mark the 100th anniversary of their founders. (g570)

■ Taking a bow, as shown in the following five images: The cast of the Spalding Gleed Boys' dramatic production of *Emil and the Detectives*, which they presented to audiences in the school hall. The week before the Gleed Girls' staged their version of A. H. Milne's *Make Believe*. (g922-6) (?)

■ Where did you get that hat? Spalding High School students dressed up for their first ever foundation fair. It was opened by Coun Mrs K. M. T. Harvey. (g527)

■ Spalding and District Boy Scouts raised nearly £180 during their Bob-a-Job week. The cash was handed over during a ceremony at Spalding Grammar School. (g1480)

This happy group of youngsters are pictured at Spalding swimming pool. Glorious weather drew more than 800 people to the pool on the opening day of the new summer season. (g1810)

Hard at work: Spalding High School art students were snapped enjoying a class in Ayscoughfee Gardens while the sun was beaming down. (g1764)

■ Spalding dancing girls Norma Gaunt, of Low Road, and Sandra White, of Acacia Avenue, both 12, added more cups to their collection when they won the open junior competition at Peterborough. Both were pupils at the Frank Will School of Dancing. (g1466)

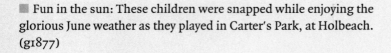

■ Fun in the sun: These children were snapped while enjoying the glorious June weather as they played in Carter's Park, at Holbeach. (g1877)

■ Outstanding features of the Holbeach Parish Church fete, held in the vicarage gardens, were country dancing by pupils at Holbeach Girls' School and a physical training display by Holbeach Boys' School. (g2175 and 2178)

1957 was the scout's year: Members celebrated the 100th anniversary of their founder Lord Robert Baden-Powell and the 50th year of scouting and guiding.

■ To mark the jubilee year the Spalding and District Boy Scouts and Girl Guides Association enjoyed a week of activities including a camp at Wyekham and a pageant at Ayscoughfee Gardens as shown in these two photographs and on the next two pages. (g1915-9 and g1954/5)

■ Fancy dress paraders: 35 children entered the event at Pinchbeck Parish Church fete. The fun and games raised £190. (g2204)

■ Ready for the off: 32 Spalding Grammar School students, accompanied by masters Mr W. A. James and Mr L. W. Dawby, waved farewell as they set off on their trip to Speyer. The party stayed at a hostel on the bank of the Rhine and made bus trips to various parts of the country. (g2439)

■ Bonjour: French scouts were given a great reception at the Vestry Hall, in Bourne, where they were staying as the guests of Mr and Mrs H. M. A. Stanton. (g2574)

■ Enjoying a final fling before the end of the school holidays – these youngsters were snapped, complete with dog, blackberrying at Spalding Marsh. (g2746)

■ Children raised the roof with their cheers at a party organised by the Battle of Britain Week committee. Around 200 youngsters from Spalding were entertained by conjouring tricks, Punch and Judy and a trampoline. They all received an ice-cream before home-time. (g2912)

Remember, remember the 5th of November: A bonfire 15ft high was the big thrill for the children of East Elloe Avenue, in Holbeach, on Guy Fawkes night. (g3499)

Ho, ho, ho – Father Christmas arrived in Spalding by boat. He climbed up the Welland bank to be greeted by milling crowds at High Bridge before pushing his way through to hold court at Berrills department store. (g3635)

■ Ahoy there! Sutton Bridge children greeted the midget submarine HMS *Sprat* as it sped along the Nene towards Wisbech (above). (g3537/g3522)

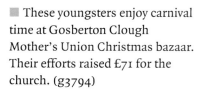 We are the champions: Paul Wakefield, a member of the Fleet School road safety quiz team, which won the junior event organised in East Elloe holds aloft the trophy. He is watched by team captain Alan Drury (14) and his team mates. (g3617)

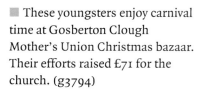 These youngsters enjoy carnival time at Gosberton Clough Mother's Union Christmas bazaar. Their efforts raised £71 for the church. (g3794)

■ Smiling faces as Spalding St Paul's wolf cub pack prepare for their party in the church schoolroom. (g3534)

■ "Think for yourselves like Lincs folk do" – that was the message to Donington Cowley School pupils on their annual speech day. Miss Casswell, a native of Quadring, handed out the prices and advice to youngsters. (g3658)

▓ Merry Christmas! Four youngsters typify the thrills for millions of boys and girls at this time of the year. This picture was taken at the Pode Hole school party. (g3958)

▓ Let them eat cake: The girls at Long Sutton senior school proudly show off their fine array of home-made Christmas cakes. (g3902)

■ Altogether, one, two, three: Dancing girls entertain the crowds at the Girls' Friendly Society Christmas Fair. (g3890)

■ Cheerio! Mr Geof Parker visited Whaplode School with his mechanical reindeer. This picture shows youngsters waving them off after their party. (g4070)

■ The old, yet ever new story of Christmas. The child in a manger at Bethlehem is depicted in these three pictures of a Nativity scene presented by the children of Pode Hole school. (g4011-3)

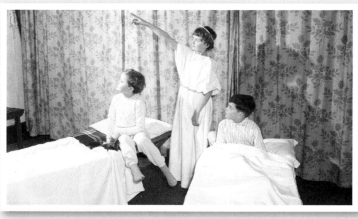

Good standards: Four out of eight youngsters who entered the Spalding Joint Road Safety Committee's cycle trials passed with flying colours. Police Sgt R. Chalkey examines the cycles on parade at Spalding. (g2354)

Sport

■ Ready for action: Spalding Grammar School's rugby first XV line up for the camera before making their way onto the pitch. (g97)

■ A hockey stick guard of honour greeted the new Mr and Mrs B. W. Gosling as they left Gosberton Clough Saint Gilbert and Hugh Church. The bride was a member of the village club. (g385)

■ Holbeach Colts fired themselves into the final of the Lincs Intermediate Cup after a 12-goal thriller against Appleby Froddingham. The final score was 8-4 to Holbeach. They went on to win the cup beating Cleethorpes 5-1. (g787)

■ Up to the 'ockey: The Ship A darts team. Messrs E. Webb, G. Brain, R. Page, J. East.
Front P. Grunnel, W. Quinton, F. Chapman and R. Riley. (g584)

■ The highly successful Pinchbeck United side were top of the senior division of the Spalding Leagues
by 13 points at the end of April, when this picture was taken. Back (from left) they were – M. Cooley,
L. Bright, S. Lambert, J. Fox, D. Fairbanks, T. Fidler. Front – G. Mayfield, R. Burgess, P. Platts,
E. Seymour and M. Hyde. (g1098/9)

Taking their eye off the ball just for a moment: Holbeach Cricket Club are pictured before they beat Sleaford by two wickets. Back (from left) – R. G. Kent-Woolsey, S. Poole, B. Keeble, J. Ambrose, C. Hale and Rev H. Skelton. Front – H. Price, J. Skate, B. Stamp, R. Jackson and R. Nurse. (g1565)

Under starter's orders: One of the events at the grasstrack meeting at Clay Lake, Spalding, gets underway. Held in Mr Ben Pearson's field, it was the first of eight evening meetings staged by the Spalding and Tongue End Auto Club. (g1646-49)

■ Three more images of the grasstrack meeting at Clay Lake, Spalding.

■ Bowled over: The Ayscoughfee Bowls Club team. Back (from left) – S. English, W. Kennedy, D. Harris, J. Spence, J. Watkin, E. Wright, D. Holmes, G. Moore. Front – B Reeve, S Parker, A. Noble and W. East. (g1997)

■ All smiles: The Holbeach Girls' School athletics team which gained outstanding success at the inter-schools sports held at Sutton Bridge. (g2278)

■ Diplomatic draw: Spalding Grammar School 1st XI took on a masters XI in an end of term cricket match. The result was a diplomatic draw. Teachers pictured here are: Mssrs Slater, B. Ford, S. Woodward, W. Hall, J. Woodward, C. Rimmel and Hornsby. Front – R. Sowett, H. Berry and K. North. (g2401)

■ Howzat! Members of Spalding Round Table and Rotary Club met each other in a cricket match at the Grammar field. Back (from left) – Mssrs H. Whitwell, R. Stanley, W.G. Hall, D. Gale, A. Coggins, L. H. Holroyde, J. Rayner, S. W. Woodward, N. Price, J. Pounder, R. Staples, J. Smith, R. Tucker. Front – D. Holmes (umpire) C. A. Nix, F. Overton, J. Dailey, S. Hickson, R. Whitson, A. Battley, P. Lamont, J. Allen and C. D. Hair. (g2353)

■ Cheering on the Tulips: A section of the crowd at the Sir Halley Stewart Playing Field watching the match between Spalding and March Town. The final result was a draw 2-2. (g2696)

■ All smiles as the Gleed School, Spalding, first eleven team lined up before their match against the combined Peterborough Schools XI. Despite putting up a good show they were beaten 4-0. (g3158)

■ Spalding United qualified for the first round of the FA Cup proper after beating Belper 1-2. Ryder scored the two goals after 34 minutes and 2 mins before the half-time interval. (g3466-73)

The last of the action against Belper
Town.

■ All the best: Councillor C. H. Peck JP,
chairman of the Urban Council wishes
Don Pickwick and his boys good luck as
they set out to play Durham in the first
round of the FA cup proper. The Tulips
lost 3-0. (g3624)

Civic and Leisure

■ Five, four, three, two, one, Happy New Year! Revellers celebrate the start of 1957 at Spalding Hockey Club's new year bash. Some traditions haven't changed, but thankfully the fashions have! (f3874)

Strictly Come Dancing at the Spalding Corn Exchange. This group of young Fred Astaires swept the board at the old-time national contest. The competition was sponsored by the Frankwill School of Dancing, Spalding. (g237/8)

■ Time for tea: Around 80 members of the Pinchbeck Darby and Joan Club were treated to tea and entertainment at the village hall. Their hosts for the afternoon were the women's section of the Royal British Legion. (g206)

■ This group of girls were picked to compete in the 1957 Miss Tulipland finals at a St Valentine's Day dance held in Long Sutton. They are (from left) Mrs E. H. Whiley, Miss Sybil Brown, Miss Margaret Faulkiner and Miss Norma Foulsham, who went on to win the coveted title. (g443)

■ The tramps supper at the Vernatts Inn, in Spalding, was a great success with all who attended dressing up to play the part. The prize for most realistic tramp went to by Mrs L. E. Houdon. (g419)

■ Timber! Fourteen chestnut trees, lining Chestnut Avenue, had to be taken down because most of them were in a dangerous condition. They were a treasured landmark in Spalding and their disappearance was said to cause deep regret, far and wide. (g413)

■ Fifty girls formed a guard of honour as Coun Mrs K. M. T. Harvey planted a tree on the site of the new Spalding High School. The historic ceremony was filmed with a cine-camera by Mr C. F. Ford. (g523)

■ Charter night: Members of Spalding Rotary Club celebrate its fifth birthday in style at Spalding Corn Exchange. (g541)

■ Encore: Spalding And District Operatic Society (SADOS) perform their version of the well-loved Gilbert and Sullivan musical *The Pirates of Penzance* at the Spalding Corn Exchang. (g597-9)

All aboard: Some of the Spalding party who visited their German twin town of Speyer, are waved off on the boat train at Spalding station by Coun E. W Dryden (third right) and Mrs Dryden, who flew over to join them later. (g786)

The thin blue line: Some of the guests at the annual dinner of the Donington section of the Special Constabulary. (g697)

■ The Spalding party made a visit to the old castle at Heidelberg during its stay in Speyer. They are back (from left) Coun W. A. Start, the Rev M. Apps, Mr K. B. Ashwell, Mr R. Stanley, Coun E. W. Dryden and Mr A. L. Tansley. Front (from left) Mr Cyril Ford, Mrs Start, Mrs Ford, Coun Mrs L Bogler (Speyer), Mrs Dryden, Mrs N. Dargel and Herr Bogler Jnr. (g755/6) (?)

■ The Tulip Time battle of the beauty attracted 16 entrants from the Spalding area. The heat winners were (front) Miss G. Tilley (19), of Pinchbeck, Miss Jennifer Knight (18) and her sister Miss Marion Knight (19), of Pinchbeck, and Miss P. Longford (18), of Spalding. Pictured at the back are judges Coun Mrs A. H. J. Hunter, Coun A. R. Ward, Mrs Dryden and Coun E. R. Dryden. (g713)

New Tulip Queen Norma Foulsham (19), of Long Sutton, receives kisses of congratulations from runners-up Pearl Longford, of Spalding, and Margaret Faulkner, of Long Sutton.

The final selection was made at a dance at Spalding Corn Exchange when the judges said Norma "was lovely, had good carriage and speech and she never appeared nervous." (g970)

Thrilled and excited: Norma was caught on camera telephoning her boyfriend in Worcestershire to share her good news. (g959)

■ Tulip Queen Norma Foulsham was crowned twice during the ceremony at Ayscoughfee. The tiara slipped off her head after Irish singer Ronnie Carroll placed it there – so he returned it and gave her a second kiss for good measure! (g1313)

■ One hundred people watched the historic ceremony for the planting of the 16 new chestnut trees in the avenue leading to Ayscoughfee Gardens, in Spalding. Christopher Sly, Coun W. A. Start, Mrs H. F. Sly, Snr scout John Rudkin, Coun E. W Dryden, rotarian R. Varney, Coun E. Fisher, Mr W. E. Cook, Mr G. S. Moore and guider Judy Clarke all took part in the occasion. (g939)

■ By Royal command: The Duke and Duchess of Gloucester, with Mr Peter Scott (right) as their guide take a tour of Peakirk Waterfront Gardens after they carried out the official opening ceremony. (g1166)

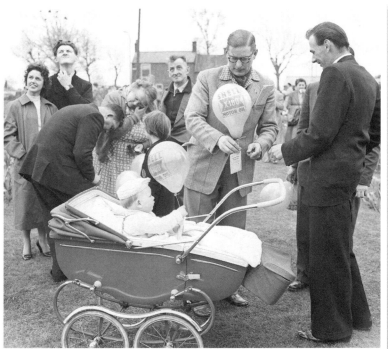

■ Holidaymakers 'blew' their petrol coupons on a trip to Tulipland. This show garden at Little London, in Spalding, was a popular venue during the event's first weekend in late-April. (G1266-9)

It's not clear what was going on in this shot. Anyone who knows can e-mail
kate.chapman@jpress.co.uk

Rogues of the road: The first tramp's supper organised by the Spalding and District Young Farmers saw every member dress as a tramp or gypsy. The title of King Tramp went to Mr T. Hardy while Miss Dorothy Seymour was Queen Gypsy. (g1086)

Nice wheels: Members of Spalding Scooter Club line up at the start of their first treasure hunt. Afterwards the organisers admitted the clues were much harder than they intended, as only one of the 15 pairs followed the right route. (g1249)

The Crowland May Day celebrations were led by Pearl Copland who was crowned in a ceremony underneath the town's May pole. She was attended by Valerie Wortley, Gillian Goodliffe, Mary Richards and Pauline Webb. (g1568 to 1572)

■ More images from the Crowland May Day celebrations.

■ A group of villagers have a go at skittle alley – one of the many sideshows at the Gosberton Clough and Risegate Youth Club fete. (g1798)

■ Summer holiday: Staff from Spalding department store Berrills pictured before they set off on their annual outing. They took a bus to Cromer for the day.

The fellowship of South Lincolnshire Servers met at St John's Spalding for solemn evensong. It was attended by representatives from three Spalding parishes, Bourne, Deeping St Nicholas, Stamford, Fleet, Lutton, Crowland, Holbeach and Sutton Bridge. Canon Lancelot Smith officiated. (g1975)

West End star Vanessa Lee told crowds at Spalding she wished she could have bought a little sunshine with her when she came to open the Big Toc H fete at the Sir Halley Stewart Field. (g1873)

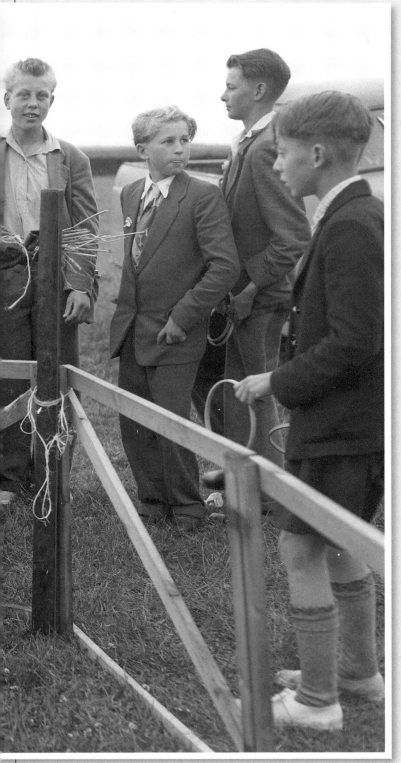

■ High jinks at Hop Pole jubilee sports and fete: Glynn Kingston, dressed as a scarecrow for the fancy dress contest, tries his hand at hoopla. He won third prize. (g2030)

■ Radio actor Bob Arnold, Tom Forrest, of Archers fame opened the United Weston Hills garden fete on the grounds of Coun F. E. Casson (right). There were stalls, side shows and a fancy dress parade. (g2134)

■ All aboard the Tydd Express: This train game was the highlight of the Tydd St Mary Parish Church fete. The event raised the record sum of £165 and was opened by Mrs Barlow, the rector's wife. (g2344)

Henry III granted a feast charter to Baston in 1257 giving it the right to hold a weekly market and yearly fair.

▣ Anyone for pork pie? Queen Ann McMonagle cut the 250lb, 6ft by 3ft giant pork pie at the 700th anniversary of Baston Feast. The pie was believed to be the largest, single pork pie ever baked and was bought by lorry from Peterborough. (G2126, G2127)

■ Everything from matching bands to horse drawn floats took part in the summer parade.

■ Local men, women, children and animals all took part in the celebrations.

David Creasey acting as Lord Abbott crowns the queen. (g2123), (g2112-2127)

■ Parking for prams was the main problem when this snap was taken of bonny babies with their mums at a baby show, at 21 Green Lane in Spalding. The proceeds went to the baptist church building fund. (g2396/2398)

■ Rain failed to stop play at the Gedney Hill Parish Church fete. Organisers and stallholders just moved everything under the cover of the church hall and carried on regardless. (g2264)

■ August sunshine favoured Pinchbeck Village Hall fete. This picture shows the ideal setting visitors had in the beautiful grounds of Otway House, the home of Colonel R. Cooke and Mrs Cooke. (g2656)

A group of happy daytrippers prepare to board their bus and leave Spalding behind for a few hours. (g2772)

The main attractions at the garden fete in Long Sutton park was an exhibition and parade of old fashioned bicycles. There was everything from the penny farthing bone shakers down to the modern day models. (g2345)

Anyone for croquet? Spalding Urban councillors and officials played a game of croquet on the lawn of their waterworks building in Manning Road, Bourne, during the annual inspection. Our picture shows town clerk Mr Raymond Hastings in action. (g3029)

These colourful scenes greeted visitors to the Broad Street schoolroom, where a Swiss evening was held. Some helpers dressed in traditional Swiss costume to help the evening go with a swing. (g3127)

Policemans' ball: A happy group pictured at Spalding Police divisions successful dance at the Corn Exchange. (g3421)

■ Happy Birthday! Guests from neighbouring womens' institutes arrived for Lutton WIs first birthday party. Mrs Baker, the oldest member, cut the celebration cake. (g3623,20,18)

A typical scene in thousands of towns and villages on Remembrance Sunday.

Pinchbeck British Legion with its banner aloft marched through the rain to the church. (g2558-62)

■ "Letting their hair down" – Rotarians give three cheers for the *Saucy Pru* in their Burlseque at Spalding Rotary Club. Members C. A. Nix, P. A. Lamont, K. Smith, C. F. Ford, A. Battley, A. Coggins and R. Varney. (g3872)

■ Dressed to impress: Some of the guests at the ball held at the Bridge Hotel, in Sutton Bridge, in aid of the Cheshire Home at Hovendon House, in Fleet. (g3807)

■ Sing in exultation: Holbeach Parish Church choir pictured as they rehearsed carols for the festive season. (g3975)

Best of the Rest

Pinchbeck Marsh Pumping Station attendant Fred Chapman found himself an unusual pet. He said this tame swan had not flown for the past three years and would only take food from him. He proved this feat in front of our photographer who snapped the bird eating from his outstretched hand. (g579)

■ Martin Waters (30) saved his own life by jumping 12 ft from a bedroom window wearing only his pyjamas and one sock, when a massive blaze broke out at his Tongue End cottage. His wife and two children were visiting relations when their home was destroyed by fire. (g782)

In these two pictures strongman Carl Dane shows off his mighty skills. It took him just under two minutes to drive a six-inch nail through two inches of wood, with just his bare fist. Not bad for a 67-year-old. (g779/80) (?)

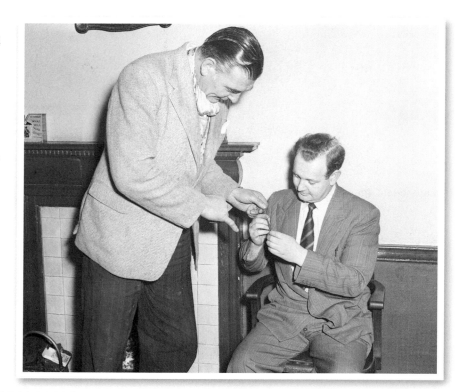

■ Honoured: Mr C. W. Ellis and Mrs E. M. Holland were recognised for the courage they showed in attempting to rescue a driver from a blazing car. They were presented with certificates for their bravery by Spalding magistrates. (g903)

■ One of the massive stone pillars of the Royce Memorial Gates, at the entrance to Ayscoughfee Hall, was shattered and one of the gates wrecked when a lorry smashed into them. Driver's mate Mr B. Mason, of Parson Drove, was thrown from the cab onto the pavement. The driver Mrs C. Horspool, fell across the seat on impact but escaped without serious injury. (g1116)

■ Here's one I made earlier: Motor mechanic Mike Davies (22) was the envy of his friends with this streamline sports car. He added a new twist to DIY when he built it himself with the help of his colleagues Tony Gibson (front right) and Derek Reynolds. (g1588)

■ End of an era: The cobblestones in Spalding Market Place disappeared. This picture shows the machine at work applying a tarmaccadam surface in Hall Place at the same time a similar operation was performed on the A17. (g2691)

Mr John Witherington grew this dahlia of Jack and the Beanstalk proportions in his back garden in Albion Street, Spalding. He said it measured about seven feet high. He had another ten which also topped the seven foot mark. (g2654)

■ Reunited: Some of the Old Boys of Moulton Grammar School and friends who gathered for their annual renunion at Moulton. (g2018)

■ A new home: Members of Whaplode Parish Council pictured at the first session at their new meeting place. (g3236)

A study in concentration: Members of Spalding Townswomens' Guild played pass the thimble at their 14th birthday party at Moose Hall. (g3652-4)

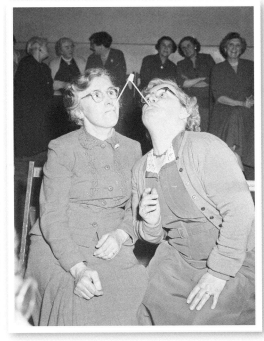

■ Twelve railway motor drivers were presented with safe driving awards for their accident free records during the past year. The presentation took place at Spalding station. (g3575)

■ Long servers: These five men were rewarded for serving 143 years between them at Bratley's Ironmongers. Mr G. Cave, Mr J. D. Glenn, Mr C. Creek, Mr C. W. F. Fieldsend and Mr H. A. Cragg. Salesman Jack Glenn notched up 40 years alone at the store. (g3765)

■ Workmen under contract to Holland County Council repair the wall and railings from Bridge Street to Vine Street. The wall was showing signs of being unsafe. This work was a temporary measure. (g3831/2)

■ Quick call the fire brigade: Spalding station officer F. C. Stamp parked his car in an alleyway near the fire station. Five minutes later he returned to find it had run into the river. A breakdown gang had to be called to pull it out. (g1436)

■ Donington firefighters were called to Sutterton Dowdyke where a Vampire jet aircraft had crashed. Officers put out the blaze but the pilot instructor was killed. (g88)

■ A US Airforce 84F Thunderstreak jet fighter crashed into the tidal mud at The Wash, near Holbeach, killing the pilot. RAF and American personnel were watched by locals at the entrance to the bombing range while attempts were made to reach the plane. (g1575)

■ The combined age of these three blacksmiths at Shepeau Stow was 221 years. The oldest of the trio was forge owner John Day, who at 88 still wielded a hammer. He is pictured with Daniel Porter (70) and his son John William Day (63). (g815)